The True Story of Fala

D0925465

The True Story of
Fala

by
MARGARET L. SUCKLEY
and
ALICE DALGLIESH

*

Illustrated with sketches by
E. N. FAIRCHILD
and
PHOTOGRAPHS

Published by Black Dome Press Corp.

in conjunction with
Wilderstein Preservation

Published by Black Dome Press Corp.
649 Delaware Ave., Delmar, N.Y. 12054
blackdomepress.com • (518) 439-6512

in conjunction with
Wilderstein Preservation
PO Box 383, Rhinebeck, N.Y. 12572

Copyright © 1942 by Margaret L. Suckley and Alice Dalgliesh

Copyright © renewed 1969 by Margaret L. Suckley and Alice Dalgliesh

Copyright © transferred from the Estate of Margaret L. Suckley to
Wilderstein Preservation 1997 and the Estate of Alice Dalgliesh

Without limiting the rights under copyright above, no part of this publication may
be reproduced, stored in or introduced into a retrieval system, or transmitted, in any
form, by any means (electronic, mechanical, photocopying, recording, or otherwise),
without the prior written permission of the publisher of this book.

ISBN: 978-1-883789-78-7

Library of Congress Card Catalog Number: 2015931604

Design: Ron Toelke Associates, www.toelkeassociates.com

Printed in the USA

10 9 8 7 6 5 4 3 2 1

My master has read this book and says that he likes it. I have put my paw mark to show that it is a true story.

Fala.

Contents

Foreword

It is a delight to welcome a new edition of *The True Story of Fala*. This is an enduring charmer of a book — fun alike for children, for dog-lovers and for older readers who can recall childhood newsreels of President Roosevelt with his celebrated Scotty. The cute drawings of Fala's high-jinks complement the historic photographs of the wartime President. Secret Service agents protecting FDR gave Fala a code name, The Informer, because to see him taking the air at the end of his leash was to know that the traveling Commander-in-Chief was aboard the nearby train.

New to this edition is an illustrated postscript about the coauthor Miss Margaret Suckley, and Wilderstein — Fala's on-again, off-again home, now a marvelously restored historic site in Rhinebeck, New York. As a cousin and neighbor of Miss Suckley, I remember playing with Rannock, the last of her Scotties and a grandson of Fala, who ruled the roost at Wilderstein sixty years ago.

May *The True Story of Fala* and tales of The Informer — the little black dog in the big white house — continue to warm our hearts for many years to come.

J. Winthrop Aldrich
Founding Board President
Wilderstein Preservation

Fala and his master

Introducing Fala

*I*t was a winter day in Washington. At the White House an important visitor was waiting to see the President.

The door opened, and a voice announced:

"THE PRESIDENT OF THE UNITED STATES."

The visitor rose—and in walked—a small black dog!

But the President was not far behind, and where the President is, there Fala his Scottish terrier is almost sure to be. This is the story of Fala, of how he came to live in the White House and to be the President's friend and constant companion.

Wendy was very proud of her puppies. There were five of them; little lively balls of fur with big heads.

Jock and Heather were fine puppies, so were the others. But one puppy, Big Boy, was more up-and-coming than all the rest. Everyone who came to look at the litter picked out Big Boy because he had such a friendly manner. They laughed at the way he staggered around on his short little legs.

Wendy took good care of her puppies. Perhaps as she washed them she told them in dog language about the things that had happened to her when *she* was a puppy. There had been one time that might have been very sad if it hadn't ended happily after all. Wendy was her mother's only puppy, and she was tiny. One day, as she played on the floor among scraps of torn newspaper, a big

gentleman came into the room and swept up the newspaper. He must have been thinking hard about something, for he never noticed the puppy, so newspapers, Wendy and all went tumbling into the ash can! Fortunately he found out his mistake and Wendy was put back in the place she came from, a little ruffled and a little puzzled at such goings on. Of course, if Wendy hadn't been saved, there never would have been any Big Boy. But there was no fear that anyone would sweep up Big Boy; *he* was much too independent.

Like most Scotties, Big Boy liked to do things his own way and in his own time. It is possible that sometimes his mother had to talk seriously to him! But he was too bright to be a really naughty or destructive puppy, and after he had chewed up his first slipper and been scolded for it, he never chewed slippers again.

The time came when all the puppies had to go to new homes. Big Boy went to live in a rambling old house in Connecticut, the house where Peter, his father, lived. Peter's mistress was allowed to choose one puppy from the litter and she took Big Boy because he seemed to have a thing called personality. Perhaps his "points" were not just right, but his eyes were bright and interested, his tail always ready to wag a welcome. He wasn't all black; a good many brown hairs showed among the black ones, especially when he had been out in the rain and his coat was wet.

The puppy did not stay long at the house in Connecticut. Peter's mistress wanted to give him to a friend of hers who lived in Dutchess County on the Hudson River, not very far from Hyde Park, the country home of the President.

"Wouldn't you like to have one of Peter's puppies, Margaret?" she asked.

Margaret hesitated a minute, then she said, "I'd love one, but you know I live in New York part of the year, and the city's no place for a puppy. He ought to go where there is grass and he can have a big yard to run in. I know just the place! The White House in Washington!"

"But—" said Peter's mistress. "Does the President *want* a dog? Of course, I'd love to give him the puppy."

"I'll ask him the next time he comes to Hyde Park,"

said Margaret. So she asked him, and the President said he'd been wanting a dog for a long time. He'd had a Scotty before named "Murray, the Outlaw of Falahill," after an ancestor of his, and he'd give the new dog the same name.

That was how Big Boy became Fala and went to live in Dutchess County.

Winter at Hyde Park

Fala's Training

*B*ig Boy—who was Fala now—traveled in a car to Dutchess County. He wasn't going straight to the President, because he was only a puppy and he had to be trained before he was ready to live in the White House.

The puppy was such a charming little roly-poly that Margaret loved him at first sight. She kept him with her all day, played with him and scolded him when he was naughty. At night he slept under her bed so that she could lean over and pat him if he got lonely. For breakfast he had an egg beaten up in milk, for supper, raw meat. He *always* wanted more! He was a strong, healthy little dog, so after a time, he ate puppy biscuits.

That was the time to teach him tricks! They made a game of it. "You give me your paw, I give you some biscuit." The puppy learned very quickly. In a short time he could give his paw, speak, roll over, lie down, and jump. He learned to "speak" quietly, for a dog that barked loudly or too often, couldn't possibly go to live in the White House.

Days were not entirely made up of lessons. Fala had two best friends, Tammy and Smudge. Smudge was such a funny dog, her mother was a Scotty, her father a spaniel, and she herself looked more like a dachshund than anything. Tammy was another Scotty. Sometimes Smudge and Fala went walking in the woods, stirring up birds and chipmunks and rabbits. Once there were three deer! Off went Fala on their trail, leaving every one very worried for fear he was too little to find his way back. But in

a short time he was back again, out of breath, wagging his tail and looking up at his mistress as if to say, "What are you worried about anyway?"

Then one day the puppy went over to Hyde Park to visit the President who wanted to get to know him a little before he took him to Washington. Fala was to stay overnight, so that the President could see what he was like and how well he got on with people.

The house was crowded with people coming and going. Fala was taken into a little room where a big man was seated at a desk. He smiled, picked the puppy up and scratched his ears, and Fala licked his chin to show that he liked it. And all of a sudden, while Fala was being petted and talked to, his mistress was gone and Fala was alone with this strange but friendly man.

The man seemed quite important. Everyone was doing things for him and calling him "Mr. President" and

asking his advice. So many people talked to the puppy and played with him that Fala was quite confused. But he was friendly and polite to everyone, even when they looked at him and made funny remarks about mops and feather dusters. "Mr. President" laughed at that and took the little Scotty up on his lap and said he was a good dog. Fala felt comfortable and safe with him, but it was a long tiring day, and he was glad when he could crawl under Mr. President's bed and go to sleep.

The next morning Fala spent most of the time under Mr. President's desk, showing how quiet and good he could be. Lots of visitors came into the office and talked with the President about many very serious things. Every once in a while he leaned over with a kind look to pat Fala and let him know he was not forgotten.

But Fala was glad when it was time to go home to Margaret. He wiggled and greeted her and smiled his funny puppy smile, curling back his lip to show his teeth.

Margaret patted him. "You are a good puppy, Fala," she said. "The President thinks you may go to live in Washington. But there are still some things you have to learn, and one of them is how to walk nicely on a city street. We shall have to go to New York and practice that."

Fala Goes to Washington

When he was six months old, Fala had his first licence tag and a new harness and leash—lovely green ones. Then he went to New York for three very tiresome weeks on the streets. He was still much of a puppy and, after running free in the country, it was hard for him to be always on the other end of a leather strap. By this time he was old enough to eat big square dog biscuits and raw meat in chunks.

Then came the day when Fala was ready to go to the White House. He had learned how to walk on the leash and not get tangled up with lamp posts or people's feet. So he was taken on the train to Washington and for the first time the puppy had to wear a muzzle. The kind baggage man took it off very soon, so that when Margaret went to the baggage car to get Fala, there he was, well and cheerful, and without the muzzle!

On the way to the White House, Margaret tried to smooth Fala's rough fur down a little.

"Fala," she said in a worried tone, "you look awfully rough and shaggy." But Fala wagged his tail and didn't worry in the least about that!

At the White House Fala saw Mr. President again— and jumped straight into his lap. Later, when the President was having tea, the puppy did all his tricks most beautifully. Margaret then left, hurrying out of the room and not looking back because she hated so to leave him.

And now Fala found himself with his new master in a house that was much bigger than any he had lived in before. Such enormous rooms, such long passages and so many people! Most of the time Fala stuck closely to his master, but sometimes his curiosity got the better of him and he just had to go exploring.

As he trotted along the halls, delightful smells came to him. Fala sniffed. In the other house those smells had meant KITCHEN. There must be a kitchen in this new house. He followed the smells down winding stairs until

Fala with his own dish

at last he came to a door that led into the largest kitchen he had ever seen.

Fala's nose twitched. "Sniff—what lovely smells!" He trotted in and begged in a most appealing way, but of course the cooks knew that puppies should not have too many tid-bits. There was a day, however, when, somehow, too many people fed Fala, and he had to pay a visit to the veterinarian. After that there was a strict rule in the White House—"Fala must not be fed, except at his own meal time."

At night Mr. President took the puppy up to his room and Fala stretched out on the rug and was soon asleep. In the morning George, the valet, came to take him out. He called softly so as not to awaken Fala's master, but the puppy wouldn't come. George thought of a plan for getting Fala quietly out of the room, and it seemed a very good plan indeed, in fact George was quite pleased with it. The next evening he tied one end of a long string to Fala's collar and one end to the door knob.

Morning came. Very quietly George opened the door and put out a hand to pull the puppy towards him. But it didn't work that way! Fala and the string had gone round and round a chair until string and chair and puppy were most hopelessly entangled. So, while George was trying to untangle the string, Mr. President woke up. He laughed when he saw what was going on and said, "Be a good puppy and go out when you're called."

Since then Fala has gone—but oh! so slowly. It takes him a whole minute to walk across the room and he doesn't yet understand why he has to go out before his master is even awake!

Outdoors

The grounds of the White House are pleasant. There are wide green lawns and shade trees and flower beds, plenty of space for a small dog to wander and sniff. There are squirrels, too, that scamper up the trees. When they see a little black dog coming they jerk their tails and chatter down at him as if they said, "Fala! Fala! Fala! Even if you *are* the President's dog you can't catch us! We lived here before you did."

Fala stands on his hind legs and tries very hard to get up to the squirrels, but they just keep chattering at him from a high, safe branch. Sometimes one gets a little too bold and comes down. Then there is a swift chase across the lawn, ending with the squirrel up in the tree once more, chattering down at Fala.

The freedom of the White House grounds didn't last long for Fala, after he had twice slipped under the gates and found his way out into the wide busy street that is Pennsylvania Avenue.

After that an enclosure was made for him near the house. Here he has shade and sun and thick grass and bushes and the squirrels come to the end of a long branch

and make faces at him because he can't chase them any more. In the enclosure there are bugs to watch, holes to be dug, and lots of birds flying in and out of every bush. It is most interesting in the spring when the birds have their nests full of hungry babies with their mouths wide open. Last spring there was a family of robins; one of the babies fell out of the nest into Fala's pen. There it lay on the grass, its wings spread, calling helplessly for its mother. Fala looked at the little thing and he must have felt sorry for it and wondered what he could do. He looked around. His house! That was the place for it. He picked up the little robin very gently and carried it carefully to the house.

Just then one of the guards happened to look over.

"What's that Fala has in his mouth?" he wondered. "Better go and see." He walked across to see what was happening. If he tried to take the bird away from the puppy it might be hurt. So the guard waited until Fala put the baby bird down on the ground, then he picked it up and examined it. Not a feather was hurt. The guard reached up and put the bird back into its nest and the robin family was happy again.

Not every morning that he spends in his yard is as exciting as this for Fala. Sometimes he just sleeps quietly in the sun, or lies and keeps one eye on those very annoying squirrels that frisk boldly about the lawn and make fun of him.

Once in a while someone has a few free moments to come and throw a ball for him to chase, or to tumble him around on the soft, green grass. Whatever may turn up, Fala is ready for it.

The portico at the White House at Christmas time

Christmas

$\mathcal{F}$ala went to live in the White House in November, so very soon after that it was Christmas. On the big north portico lighted Christmas trees twinkled and holly wreaths hung on the doors.

The festivities began two days before, when all the staff of the White House came to the President's office. The President and Mrs. Roosevelt—and of course, Fala, were there to greet them. As he shook hands with the members of the staff, the President handed each of them a package. In the package was a silver keyring with a picture of Fala on it.

Then on Christmas Eve, there was a party in the East Room of the White House. The household servants, the guards, the policemen and their families all gathered around the tall Christmas tree that sparkled with silver trimmings. Fala was there, wagging his way around among people's feet and getting lots of attention from both children and grown-ups.

After dinner Mr. President read, as he always does on Christmas Eve, to the family and guests. The story was THE CHRISTMAS CAROL by Charles Dickens. The children listened as Mr. President's deep, quiet voice read through to the words that all children love best in the story—" 'God bless us everyone,' said Tiny Tim." On the lion rug, a gift from Haile Selassie, Emperor of Abyssinia, a black puppy lay stretched out, fast asleep.

On Christmas morning, Mrs. Roosevelt was the first to get up, and she went around closing all the windows, so that the house would be warm. Then all the family gathered in Mr. President's room. Fala, two-year-old Franklin 3rd and eight-year-old Diana Hopkins ran in ahead of the others and woke the President.

"Merry Christmas! Merry Christmas!"

Then came the opening of the stockings that had been hung by the fireplace on Christmas Eve. Fala, being the youngest, got his stocking first. There was a rubber bone in it. Franklin 3rd, sitting on his grandfather's bed, opened his next with squeals and general excitement from everyone at everything that came out of it. Then Diana opened hers, and so on until it was Mrs. Roosevelt's turn. Her stocking showed the strangest bulge, somewhere in the middle. They all laughed very hard when she pulled out—a toy Scotty! The children played with it and Fala couldn't make up his mind whether this strange black dog was friend or enemy. He knew it wasn't alive, yet how could it move? The children shouted with laughter at his bewilderment. It was such fun to have a puppy to share their Christmas!

There were other pleasant happenings that Christmas day. The Crown Prince and Princess of Norway came for lunch with their three children, the Princesses Ragnhild and Astrid and Prince Harald. The Crown Princess and the children live in America since their country was invaded. Fala licked the children's bare legs,

as he loves to do and, like all others, they didn't care for the feel of his wet tongue. But they enjoyed playing with him, especially Princess Astrid, who had had to leave her own dog, an Irish setter, in Norway.

The White House seemed full of children that day. Too many children, thought Fala, as he tried to find the time to snatch a nap. There were some advantages to this day, however, for, when Fala stood on his hind legs and waved his paws in the air, he was allowed to have some little pieces of turkey. And of course he had a Christmas dinner all his own in his own special dish marked DOG.

Just Ordinary Days

After Christmas came many ordinary days on which Fala did about the same thing at the same time. Dogs love routine and come to expect it and to count on it.

Each morning George or Arthur opens the door of the President's room, calls Fala and takes him out.

When Fala comes upstairs again, he rushes into Mrs. Roosevelt's sitting room to say good-morning to her. By the fireplace stands the toy Scotty that was in Mrs. Roosevelt's stocking at Christmas time. Every morning Fala goes up to this creature and nudges it with his nose. He can never quite make up his mind about the strange dog that doesn't bark, doesn't move and doesn't even *smell* like other dogs.

After this comes one of the most important moments

in Fala's day. The President's breakfast tray is brought upstairs to his room and Fala and the tray go in together. On the breakfast tray are eggs and toast and coffee for the President, but Fala doesn't care about those things. All he can see is that fine, square dog biscuit on one side of the tray. Eyes shining, Fala puts his forefeet up on the edge of the bed, and grabs the biscuit which by this time is in his master's hand. He growls, worries the biscuit, tugs at it and proudly gets it away from Mr. President, who is, of course, trying very hard to hold on to it. Fala then carries the biscuit to the middle of the rug and finishes it down to the last crumb.

At ten-thirty Mr. President goes to his office, Fala to his pen. The morning goes by—slowly for Fala—until it is time for lunch. Mr. President usually has someone lunch with him in his office. Fala comes in.

"Hello, puppy dog!" Mr. President says. Fala wriggles and wags both ends to show how glad he is to see his master. Then he sits quietly down. He does not beg for food because his master has made it a rule that not even a guest may give him something to eat—except on *very* special occasions. Mr. Secretary Stimson had lunch with Mr. President the very first day Fala was there. Said he, "Mr. President, we have one like that at home. I warn you that *he* won't do what *you* want. *You* will do what *he* wants."

The day goes on. Mr. President is busy and Fala has learned not to ask for attention. Often he is with his master when there are important meetings. Sometimes he sits in at a Press Conference, when Mr. President talks with the newspaper men. In fact, one newspaper cartoonist made a picture of him. The newspaper men are learning at last how to spell Fala's name; with one l instead of with two.

But there is one place Fala *never* goes, and that is to

a Cabinet meeting. Important things are talked over at Cabinet meetings and a furry dog brushing against legs or licking ankles under the big table would be distracting.

Tea time at the White House is when Fala shows his best manners. If visitors pay no attention to him, he goes off to a corner and sleeps. But people like a little dog, and when they see Fala, most of them give him a pat and a kind word. Fala wags himself up to the new friend, his lip curled back in a smile. There was one visitor he especially liked. He went right up to him, standing erect on his hind feet, his front paws held as high as he could stretch them. Of course the visitor gave him some cake. Fala didn't know it was the Prime Minister of Canada! He didn't know that another visitor was the Ambassador from one of the South American republics, but made friends with him anyway.

Fala always has a friendly wag of the tail for everyone in the White House, but he makes certain demands on those he sees the oftenest. For instance, just as soon as Admiral MacIntire comes into the room, Fala sidles up to him, puts his head down on the floor sideways, then turns over on his back. The admiral knows what that means, and obediently rubs Fala's stomach. Mr. Early,

Fala at a Press conference

who is one of the President's secretaries, will take time to play with him once in a while, and Miss Le Hand, the President's private secretary, lets him lick the polish on her shoes as a great treat. Tommy Qualters, the President's bodyguard, probably has as much to do with Fala as anyone, for he goes where the President goes and it often falls to him to see that the puppy is where he is supposed to be, and that he does not get in the way.

Fala spends the afternoons out-of-doors, amusing himself as he does during the morning. When Mr. President leaves his office he picks him up on his way or sends someone to bring him in. When Fala comes into the office all full of fresh air he runs across the room, bounces onto the couch and buries his head in the pillows. The Secretaries cheer him on and he does it again and again, knowing that they are laughing *with* not *at* him. Some afternoons the President and Fala go to the swimming pool. Fala never goes into the water, but he sits and watches Mr. President swim, and licks his wet face if he comes near enough. If there are children diving and splashing, he dashes up and down along the edge of the pool. Mr. and Mrs. Roosevelt have asked many children to the pool in the White House and they have great fun there.

About half past six or seven Fala's dinner is brought in and a newspaper spread on the floor. Mr. President holds Fala's dish while Fala goes through his tricks. Then Mr. President puts the bowl down on the newspaper and Fala plunges in.

Once in a while, if things are *very* dull, Fala thinks he can liven them up by running wild for a few minutes. He dashes around the study, under chairs and tables, out into the hall, around through another room, back again to Mr. President who makes an encouraging lunge at him, off again as fast as he can go, leaving rugs turned over at the corners, and anything which can be moved out of place. Just as suddenly as he started, he stops, and collapses near Mr. President with a look out of the corners of his eyes, that says very plainly—"That's fun, why don't you do it too?"

Late in the evening Fala is asleep in Mr. President's room. He doesn't lie on a cushion, but on the rug. On hot nights he prefers the cool marble fireplace and lies there with his legs stretched out behind him, or flat on his back with all four paws in the air. Sometimes in his sleep his legs twitch as if he were running—there go those squirrels again, and in his dreams Fala is after them.

Fala Stays Behind

*I*n January came another special day, the Inauguration, when the President was to go to the Capitol to be made president for the third time.

It was a very important day and a great deal seemed to be going on at the White House. The morning began in the same way, to be sure, and Fala had his regular breakfast biscuit. But later in the day everyone was busy, and a great many people came and went.

At last Mr. President put on his overcoat and his tall silk hat. Ah, thought Fala, this means we are going for a ride. So when Mr. President went out, Fala slipped out too, and nobody noticed him. The car was waiting. Mr. President went towards it, so did Fala. The pictures tell exactly what happened and they were in all the papers.

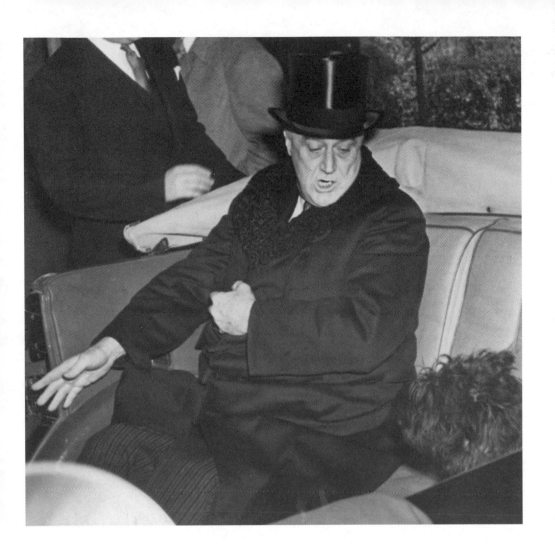

Fala: "Here I am."

Mr. President: "Sorry, old man, but you can't go this time."

Fala: "Why not? There's plenty of room."

Mr. President (firmly): "Not this time Fala; you must get out of the car."

Finally Tommy Qualters firmly lifted him out.

And into his place squeezed Senator Barkley and the
Speaker of the House!

A short time later Fala vanished from the White House. He wasn't in the house, he wasn't in the grounds. No one had remembered to put him in his pen, so he must have gone out of the gate once more.

Everyone was worried. "Where is Fala? What will the President think?"

And then a stranger appeared at the front door with the puppy in his arms. He had, so he said, picked him up at the ticket booth of a moving picture house down the street, a moving picture house that was showing films of the Inauguration! As Fala was wearing his gold-plated license tag with "Fala, the White House" on it, the man knew where to take him.

If Fala didn't get a chance to see his master made president, it wasn't long before he became a president himself. Since the war, there is a sort of dog club called Barkers for Britain which is part of Bundles for Britain. People pay for their dogs to be members of the club and the money goes to help the poor people in England whose homes have been bombed. Fala had a letter asking him to be president of Barkers for Britain and of course he accepted at once. Now he has a medal that shows he belongs to the club.

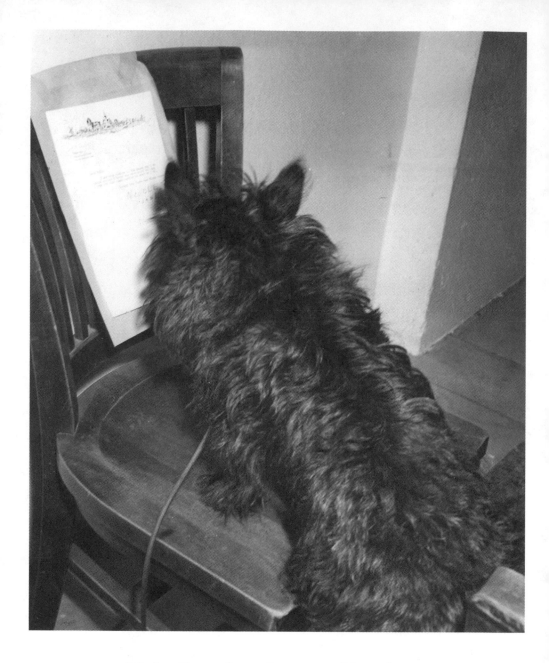

Fala "reading" one of his letters

Fala's Correspondence

Almost every dog gets a letter now and then, but Fala gets dozens and dozens of them!

Once there were pictures of him in a school paper, with a story about him. One of the pictures showed Fala standing with his front paws on the edge of a chair, "reading" a letter. Some of the children who read the story took this picture very seriously. This is what a group of first grade children wrote to the President:

Dear Mr. Roosevelt:

We saw Fala's picture in our *Weekly Reader*. Did a dog write to Fala? How can a dog write a letter? How can Fala read a letter? Can a dog really read? We hope your cold is better. We have a very nice school.

One of the nicest letters came from Hendrik van Loon. Mr. van Loon writes books, and he has stayed at the White House. Once, while he was there Fala stepped into his room and spent an hour entertaining him. A few days later Mr. van Loon sent this picture to the President.

To THE PRESIDENT — WE THANK you SiR for THE LOAN OF ONE SMALL DOG. WE DID NOT quiTE KNOW WHERE HE BEGAN AND WHERE HE ENDED BUT AS ALL OF HiM WAS perfectly

CHARMING AND FRIENDLY — HE WAS A MOST WELCOME ViSiTOR. WE HOPE THE COLD iS BETTER 2 iii '41 JiMMiE & HENDRIK VAN LOON.

When Fala became president of Barkers for Britain, the president of Bundles for Britain wrote him:

Dear Fala:

As the first dog of the U. S. A. and a leader of all loyal American canines, you will be pleased to know that we are extremely happy to have you as National President of Barkers for Britain, and the first dog to wear our medal and raise his voice in loud barks for the courageous people of Great Britain.

A letter came from a dog in Sussex, England, with a contribution of two shillings:

To Fala
The dog who owns a President
Dear Fala:

You are indeed a fine fellow to take on the Presidency of the Barkers for Britain League and I am writing to ask you if you will allow me to join it. I would indeed be very, very proud to wear your badge .... I belong to the Tail-Waggers Club, do you? Anyhow, here's a wag of the tail to a real pal,

from
Aberdeen Terrier
Beau.

Sometimes Fala gets greetings from his own family. A letter from Jock, his brother, says:

Dear Fala:

I wish that we could enjoy our birthday together, but since we can't I hope you get an extra large bone and a big dog biscuit for good luck. Just think what fun we could have playing with our brother and sister, Christopher and Heather, who are residing in our home town.

Love,

Jock

A Christmas card, with a picture of Wendy, Fala's mother, came to him on his first Christmas. It said:

Greetings, Son

Just heard you were in the White House

love from,

Mother.

These are just a few of Fala's letters. They are all kept in a file at the White House, so if at any time, Fala *should* want to read them over, he can!

WATCH YOUR STEP

Fala travels on the President's train

In the Country

*T*he most wonderful times of all are week-ends when Fala and his master go up to the big house at Hyde Park. They go in a special train with two white flags on the engine.

The first time that Fala went, Mrs. Roosevelt took him to the baggage car, perhaps because no one was sure how this new puppy would behave on the train. Now Fala rides with his master in the Pullman car.

At Hyde Park station the President's car meets them, and so does the very long, shiny black car with U.S.S.S.—United States Secret Service—on the license plates. Fala and his master get into the front seat of the smaller car, and the President drives. The Secret Service car follows. Fala sits quietly on the seat beside his master or stands up with his "elbows" on the top of the door so that he can see the country. He likes the feel of the wind and the way it blows his hair out of his eyes. Where the car goes up the long, tree-bordered driveway to the house, Fala's tail begins to wag, because he knows where he is going.

The house at Hyde Park is in very large grounds indeed, and Fala is free to wander. Off he goes, down the hill toward the river, bouncing along on his short legs, hoping that somewhere in those bushes there is a rabbit. Fala is a real out-door dog. Summer and winter, rain or shine, he wears only his own warm, shaggy coat. No blankets or sissy sweaters for a Scotsman like Fala!

Sometimes Fala and Mr. President go to a little, gray stone cottage at the top of a hill—a cottage almost hidden in the woods. There is no telephone in the cottage and not many people come there, it is a place for the President to rest and read and talk to a few friends. Fala likes to lie near Mr. President on the broad stone porch that looks away off through the trees to the Catskill mountains. When he is tired of lying still, he wanders off a little way among the tree trunks. Of course, Fala finds his way to the shiny little kitchen, for he has a friend there, the caretaker's little girl, who loves to play with him. Sometimes she plays so hard that Fala runs back to his master's side for a rest.

Then there are times when Fala goes visiting all by himself. Not far from the big house is a low gray stone building called the Library where Fala likes to go because his former mistress is there. He goes into her office and greets her. He is always very glad to see her, and she is glad that he has not forgotten her. He has a funny time in the Library, because the floors are slippery and his legs keep going out from under him. Whenever he has the time, Mr. President himself goes down to the Library. He goes around from room to room, making plans with the Director about where are to be put, and

what is to be done with the books and papers, the ship models and pictures. When he stops, down lies Fala and doesn't move again until his master goes on.

Picnics are a joy to Fala, because then everybody forgets the rules about not feeding him. When everyone is sitting on the ground eating sandwiches and fried chicken, Fala keeps his eyes on every mouthful. Sometimes his master gives him a piece of chicken and then Fala's tail wags violently. After the food is finished he wanders around looking for something to chase. Once he found the Secretary of Agriculture, who is now Vice-President, asleep behind a bush. Fala licked his ear, Mr. Wallace jumped and everybody laughed. Everyone is happy and cheerful at picnics and no one is too serious, which is one reason why Fala likes picnics so much.

All kinds of visitors, big and little, come to Hyde Park, among them the President's grandchildren. The very first time Fala had his picture taken by a newspaper man was when he was playing with the grandchildren. Kate and Sara put him across the bottom of the carriage in which sat Franklin 3rd. Just how Fala felt about it is plainly to be seen in the picture! When this picture appeared in the paper, fashionable kennels wrote to say

The President's grandchildren with Fala

that they would like to have the privilege of trimming Fala; they evidently thought he was quite a disgrace to the nation in that shaggy state. Mr. President replied, politely but firmly, that he was grateful for their interest, but Fala would remain as nature intended him to be, at least until the hot weather came.

Once two very little girls came to stay at Hyde Park; they were princesses from Holland who had had to leave their country because of the war. Princess Beatrice and Princess Irene were not used to dogs, because they had not owned one when they lived in their own country. So, when Fala came up to them, wagging a friendly tail, they were afraid.

Mrs. Roosevelt thought this would never do, so she persuaded Fala to do all his tricks for the little girls. He jumped, and begged, and lay down, and "spoke." The children were so interested they forgot to be afraid. Soon they were laughing and chasing Fala all over the room, until at last Mr. President had to pick Fala up and hold him in his arms, so the Scotty could get his breath.

A Sea-Going Dog

*F*ala's master loves the sea, so, part of the time, Fala is a sea-going dog. It is not quite so much fun on the boat as at Hyde Park because there are no rabbits or squirrels, no grass and not so much space to run. Still, Fala would much rather go with his master than stay on land.

Sometimes Mr. President and Fala spend week-ends on the yacht on the Potomac River. Sometimes they really go to sea. Once they took a long cruise in the Caribbean Sea, among the West Indian Islands, on the cruiser *Tuscaloosa*. This was quite different from being on the smooth water of the river. Some days were so rough that Fala had to be kept on his leash for fear he might fall overboard, but when the sea was smooth, he was allowed to run free and to play with the sailors. Fala is a very good sailor, but there was a long, rough night when he was so sick that he kept his master awake all night—but that wasn't Fala's fault and it never happened again.

Nights are warm in tropical seas, and one very warm night Fala had a great deal of fun. He was trotting around the deck looking at everything when suddenly he found—a whole row of bare feet. The feet belonged to sailors who were lying on the deck trying to get a cool sleep under the stars. This was too much for Fala. He licked the first pair of bare feet. The sailor jumped. Fala moved on to the next and the next and the next. It was so amusing to see the men start up with a yell out of a sound sleep! Each sailor thought it was funny, too, when

his turn was over and he could watch the others, so Fala got lots of encouragement.

One day a seaplane landed on the water near the *Tuscaloosa* and a visitor came on board. People called him "Your Royal Highness" and Fala liked the way he smiled. So he went to make friends and was patted and had his ears scratched. His Royal Highness knew exactly how to scratch a dog's ears and he told Mr. President about his own dogs, which he calls "The Gangsters."

One voyage that Fala enjoyed was the fishing trip off Florida. That was exciting. It wasn't exciting when Mr. President sat very still waiting for the fish to bite, but it was exciting when he caught one. After a time several fish lay very still on the deck.

What are those strange things, wondered Fala. He went towards them, very cautiously. Nearer—nearer—nearer, until he was only about two feet away. Flip, flop! A silvery body leapt in the air—and so did Fala. Then the game started all over again, Fala tip-toeing up to the fish, then the flip-flop and the jump. It was several days before Fala grew tired of it.

But the most important trip that Fala has taken was a secret one. On an August day he went on the yacht *Potomac* with his master, and off they sailed in a north-easterly direction. At nightfall they dropped anchor in the quiet water of an inland bay and Fala went peacefully to sleep. He wasn't at all ready to wake up when, before dawn the next morning, there was a bustle and commotion and a general feeling of hushed excitement. Fala's master showed he was excited. Before Fala knew just what was happening, he and his master and the baggage were transferred from the little *Potomac* to the big cruiser *Augusta*. Soon, as the *Augusta* steamed out to sea, the island disappeared in the distance and there was nothing but sky and ocean to be seen. The ship was full of important people—generals and admirals and colonels and captains and military and naval aides, as well as the regular officers and sailors. All of

The Tuscaloosa *leaving for the cruise*

them talked and acted as if something very unusual were happening. For once the newspaper men were not there to write a story about what did or did not happen every minute. Fala took it all calmly and wandered about the deck making friends with the sailors as usual.

That night there was a little fog, but the next morning all was clear again. Fala and his master sat on the upper deck, away up in the bow, and enjoyed the spray blowing in their faces. For Fala and his master are true sailors, they love the smell of salt water and Fala licks his lips to get the salty taste. Perhaps his master does, too, when nobody is looking.

All that day the ship, with other escorting cruisers, plowed through the water, throwing a sheet of spray to each side and leaving a white trail of foam behind. On and on through the days and through the nights.

Then the *Augusta* dropped anchor in a harbor with high mountains on every side. Fala's master said it looked liked the fjords in far-off Norway.

For a couple of hours Mr. President had a quiet time fishing—and then things weren't quiet any more. Other people came to the ship and there was talking and planning. Something was going to happen!

Then came Saturday morning. No one had any time to play with a dog or even say a few friendly words to him. Fala went slowly and sadly up to the bow; perhaps his master would join him there. He sat all alone, looking out to sea. And then—a huge ship came steaming into the harbor. She came close to the *Augusta* and dropped anchor.

Four days followed during which Mr. President had not a moment to play with his dog. The Prime Minister of Great Britain had come on the big ship *Prince of Wales* and with him were his own generals and admirals and colonels and captains and aides. Fala's master entertained them on the *Augusta* and the Prime Minister entertained Mr. President on *his* ship. The Prime Minister likes cats, he has one at home in London called Nelson, and he even stopped to pet the ship's cat of the *Prince of Wales* when he left to go on board the *Augusta*. Perhaps it was because he likes cats that he didn't notice Fala at first, perhaps it was just because he was thinking of important things. At dinner time Fala was determined that the Prime Minister should pay a little attention to him, especially as the Prime Minister was eating hors d'oeuvres that looked and smelled simply delicious. So

Fala lay down and rolled over. Nothing happened. Then Fala did his trick that seldom fails, he stood on his hind legs and waved his paws beseechingly. That worked!

The days were dull and lonely for Fala. Of course his master saw to it that he had his supper as usual, and at night Fala slept in Mr. President's cabin. The rest of the time Fala wandered by himself while people talked for long hours behind closed doors. Voices were serious but friendly, for everyone was working for the same thing.

At last one afternoon Fala had his master's attention for a little while. The President and the Prime Minister were waiting to be photographed. They sat in chairs on the deck surrounded by the admirals and generals and captains and aides, for this was to be an important and historic picture—the first time that a President of the United States and a Prime Minister of Great Britain had met at sea to talk over matters important to both their countries. The photographers were just going to click their cameras, when the President spied a drooping little bundle of fur wandering sadly among the many legs on deck.

"Here, Fala, come into the picture," he called. The bundle of fur suddenly became a happy and cheerful dog as Fala came trotting over. He sat at his master's feet and faced the camera in approved style, never stirring until the picture was taken. That was how he happened to be in a picture which children in years to come may see in their history books.

In the days and weeks that followed, Mr. President was very busy. Fala heard him talking seriously with many people, and often he looked worried and troubled. One of the busiest times of all was when the Prime Minister of Great Britain came again to meet with the President and to talk over what their countries would do to work together in the war. This time the Prime Minister stayed at the White House and he and Fala got to know each other better.

The President has great responsibilities now and it is well that Fala is an understanding and patient companion. Not long ago a letter came to him from his Scotty cousin, Jock Murray, who lives across the ocean:

Fala has his place in an important photograph

"To our wee brither Scot, Fala o' Falahill.

"You are a lucky boy, Fala. Give all you have to make your master happy, and always wag your tail. He has big heavy burdens to carry, and parcels, what the humans call 'burdens and responsibility'—you can sometimes help to carry them."

And this is just exactly what Fala is doing.

About Margaret Suckley

Margaret L. Suckley was the sixth cousin, a close friend, and confidante of Franklin Delano Roosevelt. She trained and presented Fala to FDR, and offered a glimpse into Fala's exciting world as "First Dog" with the publication of *The True Story of Fala* in 1942.

Miss Suckley was a frequent guest at the White House, helped to establish the FDR Library in Hyde Park, and was at the President's side in Warm Springs when he died. Her collection of letters they exchanged and extensive diaries are one of the best surviving records for understanding the private side of Roosevelt's life during this period.

Margaret Suckley lived at Wilderstein, the beloved Suckley family home in Rhinebeck, New York. Located just a few miles north of Springwood, Franklin Roosevelt's family home, Wilderstein is now a historic house museum with 40 acres of grounds and trails open to the public. The estate, with its exquisite Queen Anne mansion and Calvert Vaux-designed landscape, is widely regarded as the Hudson Valley's most important example of Victorian architecture.

Margaret Suckley with President Roosevelt aboard the Potomac *in 1937.*

Fala spent much time with Margaret Suckley and at Wilderstein. He lived there for six months during his obedience training, and stayed with her regularly when FDR and Eleanor Roosevelt were unable to have him along on their travels. While Fala was a puppy, Miss Suckley taught him the repertoire of tricks he later used to entertain dignitaries and the press. She also looked after Fala whenever she visited or accompanied the President. Among her greatest pleasures and most cherished duties was taking Fala for his walks.

Fala sits with Margaret Suckley outside the FDR Presidential Library where she was employed as an archivist for twenty years. Photograph circa 1941.

Margaret Suckley and Fala seated on a couch in FDR's study at the White House, 1942.

Right: FDR at Top Cottage with Fala and the granddaughter of his Hyde Park caretaker. This rare photograph of FDR in his wheelchair was taken by Margaret Suckley in 1941. Below: Margaret Suckley at Wilderstein in 1945 with her Scotty dog Button and two puppies sired by Fala.

Margaret Suckley with a later Scotty on a bench at Wilderstein in 1957.

Margaret Suckley in her nineties in front of Wilderstein circa 1985.

Wilderstein Historic Site

Tours

Wilderstein's regular season for guided house tours is May to October, Thursday through Sunday, from noon until 4pm. Wilderstein is also open for holiday tours on Thanksgiving weekend and all weekends in December. Group tours may be arranged at any time by advance reservation. Visitors are welcome to explore Wilderstein's grounds and trails year-round, daily, from 9am to 4pm.

Supporting Wilderstein

Please help to sustain Wilderstein by joining as a member of the growing family of annual contributors. As an independent not-for-profit historic site, Wilderstein would not exist without the dedicated support of its members, volunteers, and community partners. The operation and ongoing preservation of Wilderstein is an immense collective effort possible only through the generosity of the public. For information about membership, please contact Wilderstein Historic Site.

Contact Information

Street Address: 330 Morton Road — Rhinebeck, NY 12572
Mailing Address: PO Box 383 — Rhinebeck, NY 12572
Telephone: 845.876.4818
Website: www.wilderstein.org

Acknowledgments

Color photograph used on the cover by permission of
This Week magazine.

Margaret Suckley took the informal photograph of the President
and Fala which is used as a frontispiece.

The photographs on pages 6, 20, 29, 34, 35, 36, 38, 49, 55, 61 are
used by permission of the Press Association.

The photograph on page 13 is used by permission of *Life* magazine.

The photographs on pages 33, 44 are used by permission of
UPI/Corbis-Bettmann.

The medal on page 41 is used by permission of the Bundles for
Britain.

The photographs on pages 63, 64, 65, 66, 67 are courtesy
of Wilderstein Preservation.

The photograph on page 68 is by Shel Secunda.

Special thanks to the FDR Presidential Library in Hyde Park,
New York.